Nikki Giovanni in the Classroom

Nikki Giovanni in the Classroom

"the same ol danger but a brand new pleasure"

The NCTE High School Literature Series

Carol Jago
Santa Monica High School

NATIONAL COUNCIL OF TEACHERS OF ENGLISH
1111 W. KENYON ROAD, URBANA, ILLINOIS 61801-1096

We gratefully acknowledge William Morrow & Company, Inc. who generously gave us permission to reproduce the following material:

"I Plant Geraniums" from *Racism 101*, copyright 1994; fourteen poems from THE SELECTED POEMS OF NIKKI GIOVANNI, compilation copyright 1997; two poems from LOVE POEMS by Nikki Giovanni, compilation copyright 1997.

Cover photo by Barron Claiborne. Reprinted with permission,

Staff Editor: Zarina M. Hock
Editorial Assistant: Jessica L. Creed
Interior Design: Jenny Jensen Greenleaf
Cover Design: Jenny Jensen Greenleaf

NCTE Stock Number: 52120-3050
ISSN 1525-5786

It is the policy of NCTE in its journals and other publications to provide a forum for the open discussion of ideas concerning the content and the teaching of English and the language arts. Publicity accorded to any particular point of view does not imply endorsement by the Executive Committee, the Board of Directors, or the membership at large, except in announcements of policy, where such endorsement is clearly specified.

Library of Congress Cataloging-in-Publication Data
Jago, Carol, 1951–
  Nikki Giovanni in the classroom: "the same ol danger but a brand new pleasure"/ Carol Jago.
    p. cm.—(The NCTE high school literature series)
  ISBN 0-8141-5212-0
  1. Giovanni, Nikki—Study and teaching (Secondary) 2. Afro-American women in literature—Study and teaching (Secondary) 3. Afro-Americans in literature—Study and teaching (Secondary)
  I. Title. II. Series.
  PS3557.I55Z464 1999
  811'.54—dc21
                                                              99-36770
                                                                   CIP

"If I could come back as anything I'd be a bird, first, but definitely the command key
is my second choice."

−Nikki Giovanni

Contents

This chapter describes how teachers can integrate Nikki Giovanni's poetry into the traditional curriculum, pairing poems thematically with commonly taught novels and plays. Ideas for use of this poetry in cross-curricular or interdisciplinary projects included.

Additional sources of information about Nikki Giovanni and her work.

The NCTE High School Literature Series

■ ■

Apart from Emily Dickinson, Langston Hughes, and Mark Twain, few writers stand out as individuals in students' minds. Why should they? Teenagers seldom come across actual books of poetry or collections of stories by a single author. Even avid readers who have devoured every word of J. R. R. Tolkien's trilogy and all six of Douglas Adams's *Hitchhiker's Guide to the Galaxy* books, and who can recognize a page of Stephen King in a heartbeat, rarely have the same sense of recognition or love for a poet or short-story writer.

The reason has partly to do with instruction. More often than not, teachers serve students a smorgasbord of poems and stories, hoping that one will pique their appetite for more. Rather than developing a deep knowledge of a particular writer's work, students emerge with the vague sense that some poems and stories are "pretty cool" while others are "boring." This is the not the kind of experience that makes for a lifelong love of the genre.

Textbook anthologies promote this topsoil approach to teaching poetry by scattering various poems, most often quite short and "multicultural," throughout their tomes, using verse to provide visual relief for the reader between longer prose excerpts. But poetry does not belong in a sidebar. And a few poems by Native Americans do not create a diverse collection of voices. What can offer balance to a traditional curriculum is the in-depth study of contemporary poets. When students read a collection of poems or stories by one author, written over many years and in a variety of moods and historical moments, they begin to determine for themselves what is unique about a writer, what makes him or her worthy of the exalted title, "artist."

As a classroom teacher working in a public urban high school, I know first hand the challenges involved in teaching literature to today's students. I know, too, that without powerful stories and poems to engage them, many will never acquire the literacy skills taxpayers and politicians praise so highly.

One-third of the students at Santa Monica High School are English-language learners. There are over twenty different languages spoken on campus. Our student body includes children who live in million-dollar homes and others who reside in homeless shelters. Diversity isn't something we work to achieve. What we work on is harmony.

Reading and writing poetry helps us to find the notes we share. My students have loved the literature in this series. I think yours will, too.

CAROL JAGO
Santa Monica High School
Santa Monica, California

Introduction

"the same ol danger but a brand new pleasure"

Nikki Giovanni's career as a writer has spanned more than a quarter of a century from the revolutionary sixties, where she first emerged as a voice for her times. Her first book of poems, *Black Feeling, Black Talk,* includes "The Funeral of Martin Luther King, Jr."

> His headstone said
> FREE AT LAST, FREE AT LAST
> But death is a slave's freedom
> We seek the freedom of free men
> And the construction of a world
> Where Martin Luther King could have lived
> and preached non-violence

Giovanni's 1997 collection, *Love Poems,* is dedicated to Tupac Shakur (1971–1996), "a lover whose love was often deliberately misunderstood but who will live in the sun and the rains and whose name will echo through all the winds whose spirit will flower and who like Emmett Till and Malcolm X will be remembered by his people for the great man he could have become and most especially for the beautiful boy that he was."

When I read this introduction to my class, students tripped over one another to get to the book. Who was this old lady who knew about Tupac? What they found was "All Eyez On U," a stream-of-consciousness poem about Tupac Shakur by Giovanni:

there are those who wanted to make *him* the problem
   who wanted
to believe if they silenced 2Pac all would be quiet on the ghetto
front there are those who testified that the problem wasn't the
  conditions
but the people talking about them

they took away band so the boys started scratching they took away
gym so the boys started break dancing the boys started rapping
cause they gave them the guns and the drugs but not the schools an
libraries

what a beautiful boy to lose

You don't need to be an aficionado of rap music or a fan of Tupac Shakur to see the teaching potential in these lines. One of the first things my students worried over was how this could be a poem when it "doesn't look like one or anything." It doesn't. But what qualifies Giovanni's text as poetry is its power-per-word quotient. Like all good poetry, these lines say more, and say it more intensely than ordinary language.

In *Sound and Sense,* Laurence Perrine defines poetry as "something central to existence, something having unique value to the fully realized life, something that we are better off for having and spiritually impoverished without" (1991, 3). I asked students if they thought Nikki Giovanni's poetry met this criterion. The rest of this volume is dedicated to their answer.

1 Where Life and Art Intersect

When her poetry first emerged from the Black Rights Movement in the late 1960s, Nikki Giovanni became almost at once a celebrated and controversial voice for her times. Born in Knoxville, Tennessee, in 1943 and named Yolande Cornelia Giovanni Jr., she was one of the first black poets to achieve stardom. *Black Feeling, Black Talk,* her first book, is a slim volume of revolutionary poems full of passion, anger, frustration, and love. Giovanni wrote these poems while enrolled in the Master of Fine Arts program at Columbia University. One of the purposes of the program was to publish a book. Giovanni completed *Black Feeling, Black Talk,* published it, and then dropped out of the program, figuring that she had fulfilled the program's requirements. In an interview for *Writer's Digest* (February 1989, 33), Nikki Giovanni describes her Cinderella story:

> To get publicity for *Black Feeling, Black Talk,* I got the idea to have a book party at Birdland because I love jazz. I went to see Harold Logan, who was the manager, and said, "Hi, I'm Nikki Giovanni. I'm a poet, and I have a new book, and I'd love to have a book party at Birdland. I know you're dead on Sundays, so that would be a good day. What do I have to do to have a party here?"
>
> He looked at me like I was crazy, but he finally said, "I'll tell you what. You bring me 125 people and you can have the club. But if you bring me 124 people or any less, you owe me $500."
>
> I said, "Fine," but afterward I thought how would I get $500

if I failed. That was a huge amount of money for me in 1969. Anyway, I make up invitations and sent them out to all sorts of groups and that cost me a couple of hundred dollars to start. Then I contacted radio stations and asked if I could go on the air to talk about my book party. I figured the midnight audiences are full of readers, so I did a lot of late night shows. I did everything I could do free to ask people to come to Birdland for my book party. I even asked friends like Morgan Freeman, who was a young actor at the time to read from my book and we'd have a kind of Sunday cabaret.

I ended up with a crowd at Birdland that snaked all the way down the street and turned the corner. Birdland is right in the backyard of *The New York Times,* so some reporters happened to look out the window and wondered what the crowd was all about, and came down to investigate. When they found out everyone was there for a poetry reading, they knew they had a story.

The New York Times took a picture of me, which wound up on the front page of the metro section and, because of the publicity, I sold 10,000 books in the next eight months and attracted the attention of some major publishers.

If this sounds like a Cinderella story, remember I made my own slipper. I'm a Midwesterner. I was raised in Cincinnati, and one of the things I think Midwesterners do very well is work hard. We don't expect magic; we make magic.

Between 1967 and 1970, Giovanni published three books of poetry that achieved wide readership in the black community: *Black Feeling, Black Talk* (1967), *Black Judgment* (1968), *Re: Creation* (1970). These early poems are cultural artifacts of those troubled times. The boldness of her revolutionary proclamations and the accessibility of her poems made these volumes big hits on the poetry charts. Displaying not only an entrepreneurial spirit but also a keen awareness of the Black Aesthetic claim that poetry cannot be divorced from music in the African American tradition, Giovanni made several albums of her poetry read in musical settings, some with religious choirs, others with jazz musicians.

But by the early 1970s, the poetry of the Black Revolution had exhausted its market. At the same time, the subject matter for Nikki Giovanni's poetry began to broaden. In 1972, she produced an electric collection of love poems called *My House* which was followed by *The Women and the Men* in 1974. Both brought her critical acclaim and remain in print as single volumes, remarkable testimony to the enduring attraction of these poems to readers.

One of Giovanni's early poems, "Nikki-Rosa," foreshadows the themes that animate the best of her work both early and late. In it, Giovanni describes specific moments from her own childhood. But the images she recalls are more than biographical details; they are evidence to support her premise that growing up black doesn't always mean growing up in hardship.

Nikki-Rosa
Nikki Giovanni

childhood remembrances are always a drag
if you're Black
you always remember things like living in Woodlawn
with no inside toilet
and if you become famous or something
they never talk about how happy you were to have your mother
all to yourself and
how good the water felt when you got your bath
from one of those
big tubs that folk in chicago barbecue in
and somehow when you talk about home
it never gets across how much you
understood their feelings
as the whole family attended meetings about Hollydale
and even though you remember

your biographers never understand
your father's pain as he sells his stock
and another dream goes
And though you're poor it isn't poverty that
concerns you
and though they fought a lot
it isn't your father's drinking that makes any difference
but only that everybody is together and you
and your sister have happy birthdays and very good
Christmasses
and I really hope no white person ever has cause
to write about me
because they never understand
Black love is Black wealth and they'll
probably talk about my hard childhood
and never understand that
all the while I was quite happy

Prereading

Before reading "Nikki-Rosa," ask students to describe what they envision when they say or hear that someone has had a "hard childhood." Create a cluster on the board of all the features of this condition from your students' point of view.

Then ask students to think about some of the things they experienced as children that might make someone feel sorry for them but that were actually pleasurable. Students are likely to recall having to share a bed with a sibling where there was plenty of squabbling over space but also many sweet secrets shared. Or a student might remember weekly chores like ironing her father's shirts which, though she would never admit it to her mother, made her feel closer to her dad. Students might offer memories of hand-me-down clothes, errands to the store, or left over dinners. Make a list of these on the board and title them "Childhood Remembrances." Save this list.

Reading

Read "Nikki-Rosa" aloud to students and then ask them to read it again to themselves silently. When you feel certain students have done this, have them read the poem a third time, underlining or highlighting all the words and phrases that describe the various pleasures the speaker in the poem remembers experiencing in her "hard" childhood.

Remind students that while this poem may seem to be obviously autobiographical—the title is reasonably strong evidence—a careful reader always considers the speaker in a poem to be separate from the author.

Discussion

To initiate a discussion of this poem, you might want to ask students the following questions. Encourage the discussion to roam where it will, rather than sticking to this list. Remember, *requiring* students to answer these questions (especially in complete sentences) could probably make them hate the poem forever.

- Did any of the phrases you marked in "Nikki-Rosa" remind you of your own childhood experiences? How did that make you feel about what you read?

- How would you describe the speaker's attitude toward her childhood? Why do you think she is worried that a biographer will "never understand"?

- What do you think you "understand" about the circumstances of the speaker's childhood? (Push students to be very specific here in order to help them recreate the world in which these childhood remembrances existed.)

- Why do you think Nikki Giovanni chooses to address the reader directly as "you"? What effect did this have on you as a reader? What assumption does this use of the second person make about Giovanni's expectation of who her readers will be?

- How did you interpret the line "And though you're poor it isn't poverty that / concerns you"? If it wasn't poverty that concerned the speaker, what was it that concerned her? (I think it is *joi de vivre* that has always animated Nikki Giovanni as a child, as an adult, and as a poet; but that is only one reader's response and not necessarily what your students will read into this line.)

Potential Minefields

The line "and I really hope no white person ever has cause / to write about me / because they never understand" might cause some students to feel that Nikki Giovanni is casting them as the "bad guys" in this poem. Encourage students to think about how Nikki Giovanni's experience as a black person might lead her to make this generalization about white people. Discourage students from relegating such generalizations to the "bad old days" before the Civil Rights movement. If the issue comes up, it is important to discuss the pervasive presence of racism in our own society and how this shapes our generalizations about who we expect will "understand" us and who we expect never will.

Writing

Here is a suggested sequence of activities:

Gathering material: Bring out the list of childhood remembrances that students compiled as a class and ask them to take out a piece of paper and make a list that is uniquely theirs. Let students know that no one need ever see this list and that they should simply try to record as many occurrences from their child-hood that they can remember, both important and seemingly in-consequential.

Talk as prewriting: Put students into pairs and have them take turns imagining that they are biographers conducting an inter-view with a famous person in order to write a book about this person's life. This particular interview should focus on childhood remem-brances. When the first interview is complete, students should re-verse roles.

Before they begin, make sure students understand exactly what a biography is. For students with limited experience of the genre, borrow an armload of biographies from the school library and let them browse. They need to see the kind of detail biographers include when writing about a famous person's life. If your stu-dents are like mine, biographies of sports figures, rock stars, and celebrities like Selena will get their attention more readily than *The Life of Amelia Earhart.*

Writing to explore an idea: Have students imagine that they are back home following the interview with their biographers. Ask them to write a diary entry for the day describing how they felt about being interviewed and what they hoped their biographer "understood" about the childhood remembrances they had de-scribed. Suggest that students make references to Nikki Giovanni's poem "Nikki-Rosa" in their diary entry if it seems appropriate.

An Oral History Project: Now that students have some famil-iarity with the interview process, brainstorm a list of adults they might like to interview about childhood memories. When every-one has a person in mind, create a list of questions that students could ask. Effective interview questions should invite the person being interviewed to muse on his or her experiences; they should not be yes/no or fill-in-the-blank questions. Given that students will be the ones asking the questions, it is vital that they be written in their own words. I have listed a few to seed students' thinking but urge you to encourage your students to come up with their own.

- What do you remember most about your childhood?
- Why do you think this memory has stayed with you?
- What places come to mind when you think about being a kid?
- What people?

If the technology is available, have students tape the interviews and then play them for one another to identify the most evocative details. These will then become the idea seeds for a poem that demonstrates how life and art intersect.

Formal writing assignment: Ask students to select particularly revealing and interesting details from their interviews and then to tease these words and phrasings into a poem. Their drafts may take the form of a story poem in which the writer describes an event from beginning to end. They may also imitate "Nikki-Rosa" and use a series of moments to create a picture of childhood. When students are satisfied with their drafts, have them turn to partners for help with revision. If possible, suggest that students show this draft to the person they interviewed to see if it is true to what they were told. Encourage students to type their poems and present a polished copy to the adult whose history they have tapped.

Autobiography as Art

Nikki Giovanni's essay "On Being Asked What It's Like to Be Black," first appeared in 1969 in *US* and was later reprinted in *Gemini: An Extended Autobiographical Statement on My First Twenty-Five*

Years of Being a Black Poet. Here Giovanni employs a different genre to explore the themes of "Nikki-Rosa." As this essay—written when she was twenty-five years old—demonstrates, Giovanni was outspoken from the start. It also foreshadows the extraordinary lady she has become.

> I've always known I was colored. When I was a Negro I knew I was colored; now that I'm Black I know which color it is. Any identity crisis I may have had never centered on race. I love those long, involved, big-worded essays on "How I Discovered My Blackness" in twenty-five words more or less which generally appear in some mass magazine—always somehow smelling like Coke or Kellogg's corn flakes—the prize for the best essay being a brass knuckle up your head or behind, if you make any distinction between the two (24).

The article goes on to describe her family history and the kind of people who Giovanni feels helped to make her who she is.

> Now, Mommy was an intellectual, aristocratic woman, which in her time was not at all fashionable. She read, liked paintings, played tennis and liked to party a great deal. Had she been rich she would have followed the sun—going places, learning things and being just generally unable to hold a job and be useful. But Mommy made just one bad mistake in the scheme of things—she sashayed across the Knoxville College campus, hair swinging down to her behind, most probably carrying a tennis racket, and ran into a shin-head Negro with a pretty suit on. He, being warm and friendly and definitely looking for a city girl to roost with, introduced himself. I have always thought that if his name hadn't been exotic she would never have given him a second thought; but Grandfather, whom my mother was so much like, had a weakness for Romance languages and here comes this smiling dude with Giovanni for a name. Mommy decided to take him home (28–29).

In the final paragraph, Giovanni explains:

> I was trained intellectually and spiritually to respect myself
> and the people who respected me. I was emotionally trained to
> love those who love me. If such a thing can be, I was trained to
> be in power—that is, to learn and act upon necessary emo-
> tions which will grant me more control over my life. Some-
> times it's a painful thing to make decisions based on our train-
> ing, but if we are properly trained we do. I consider this a
> good. My life is not all it will be. There is a real possibility that
> I can be the first person in my family to be free. That would
> make me happy. I'm twenty-five years old. A revolutionary poet.
> I love (33).

Turning Students' Own Lives into Art

Though born in Knoxville, Tennessee, Nikki Giovanni's family
moved to Cincinnati, Ohio, shortly thereafter. Giovanni returned
to her birthplace often and spent most summers and holidays
with her grandparents and extended family. As this poem dem-
onstrates so beautifully, wherever she traveled, Knoxville remained
her true home.

Knoxville, Tennessee [1]
Nikki Giovanni

I always like summer
best
you can eat fresh corn
from daddy's garden
and okra
and greens
and cabbage
and lots of
barbecue
and buttermilk
and homemade ice-cream

at the church picnic
and listen to
gospel music
outside
at the church
homecoming
and go to the mountains with
your grandmother
and go barefooted
and be warm
all the time
not only when you go to bed
and sleep

After reading this poem aloud, I ask students what they can tell about the speaker from the things Giovanni has chosen to list as what she likes best. Invariably students identify the speaker as black and from the country. I push them to think about what they can tell from the poem about her attitudes, about what they think might be her priorities in life.

I then invite students to write a poem of their own about something, someplace, or someone they like best. My instructions are intentionally vague though I suggest that they use short lines and imitate the list-like quality of Giovanni's poem. Students soon find that they like this technique very much. With very few words they can produce a page full of poetry. I remind them that in order for their poem to replicate the power of Giovanni's poem, their few words must be exceptionally well-chosen.

As students share their poems with the class, we talk about how it feels to use details from their own lives as raw material for their art. Though at first some think I go too far to equate what they have written with what "real poets" create, the more we look for distinctions between *their* best work and published poetry, the more their objections subside. Life and art intersect in the classroom as well as on stage or in a published volume. Witness their work:

917 Kings Road

I always liked grandma
best
you can bathe
in her thick love
and borscht
and babka
and blintzes
and lots of
homemade pickles
sultry stews
and super sweets

at the dinner table
and listen to Russian radio
inside
where it is always warm
on the couch
and be lost in papa
as he strums his guitar
plays his voice
sings his memories
of how he always
liked grandma
best
—*Edward Brodsky*

I have no idea why so many students chose to center their poems on the page, but they did, this one to form a Christmas tree:

LA, California

I
always love
Christmas time best.
You go out with your family
Looking for the perfect tree. Coming home
and decorating it,
and watching it grow even more
beautiful as each decoration is added. Waiting for
the special moment when the lights come on. Fascinated with
all the new colors in
the room: red, green, blue, silver.
Going to sleep at nine so I could wake up to
hide the presents before the family wakes up. Anxious
to know what is
under the tree for me. Thanking God over
and over for giving me another Christmas with the
people
I love.
—Angelin Rahnavardan

I always like winter
best
when it is really cold
and I drink hot chocolate
with creamand sugar
and a little bit of honey

I love when it snows
I go outside and have a snowfight
with my friends
go skiing
It is the only time when hiding under
grandma's brown blanket
with a cup of hot tea
feels good and warm
and sleepy
—Farzad Nikmanesh

I always love writing music
Best
Walking to the corner market
And a melody
Pops into my body
And I race home
Singing out loud
Forgetting about the Bisquick
Running into my room
And putting chords down

Sometimes sitting on my bed
Playing the same thing
Over and over
And over
Squeezing out life from a half dead tune

Jammin in Zack's garage
With the amps at eleven
And we're funky
And we're grooving
And then we take
The groove to
The Roxy
Or the Troubadour
Or an all-girls school dance

And afterwards some people are impressed
And afterwards some people say "that sucked"
And afterwards I am impressed
And afterwards I say "that sucked"
And I get discouraged
And never want to write music again

But I'm always writing music
No matter where I am
Or who I'm with
Even if I'm with Susannah

I always like writing music
best
—*Alexi Glickman*

Then of course there are the students who take an assignment like this one and run with it in a direction the teacher never imagined:

I always like it when I see a pretty girl
You can look at her body
and smile
and legs
and breasts
And her beautiful hair that just makes
You want to go over and start making love to her.

When I meet a girl
I always put a new piece of gum in my mouth
I tell her what she wants to hear
even if it's not completely
true
I give her a few compliments
so she feels special
And after that
As long as she doesn't think you're ugly
you're in there
if you know what
I mean
—*Tony Gallo*

There is no doubt in my mind that these 17-year-olds understand how life and art can intersect. Nikki Giovanni's simple celebration of the things that she likes best inspired them to look inside their own lives for poetic possibilities.

The Evolution of the Artist

Toward the end of her militant period, Nikki Giovanni wrote "Revolutionary Dreams." In this poem she explores the development of her thinking in ways that help students see how changing one's mind need not invalidate the authenticity of what has been said and written earlier. In fact, it shows growth.

Revolutionary Dreams
Nikki Giovanni

i used to dream militant
dreams of taking
over america to show
these white folks how it should be
done
i used to dream radical dreams
of blowing everyone away with my perceptive powers
of correct analysis
i even used to think i'd be the one
to stop the riot and negotiate the peace
then i awoke and dug
that if i dreamed natural
dreams of being a natural
woman doing what a woman
does when she's natural
i would have a revolution

Like much of Giovanni's later poetry, "Revolutionary Dreams" continues to advocate change but views revolution as a personal rather than a collective movement. She has said that "the fight in the world today is the fight to be an individual" (NCTE Annual Convention, November 1998).

Further Resources

■ For more information about Nikki Giovanni's place within the tradition of African American literature, see *The Norton Anthology of African American Literature* edited by Henry Louis Gates Jr. and Nellie Y. McKay. The volume was first published in 1997. If your school library doesn't have it yet, they should.

■ No formal biography of Nikki Giovanni has yet been published, but if students are interested in learning more about her life, I send them to Giovanni's own collection *Gemini: An Extended Autobiographical Statement on My First Twenty-Five Years of Being a Black Poet* (1976).

Note

1. Artist Larry Johnson has illustrated "Knoxville, Tennessee," and the collaborative work of poet and painter has been published by Scholastic as a children's picture book (ISBN 0-590-47074-4).

2 Looking at Language

■ ■

Most students consider the formal study of poetry the epitome of school for school's sake. They contend that nobody apart from the odd English teacher cares a jot about literary devices or figures of speech. My students complain all the time.

"Can you imagine Oprah having a program on *onomatopoeia*, Mrs. Jago? I mean, really, you're tripping."

"Maybe I am, Ross. But look at the phrase you just used. When you said that I was 'tripping,' you used figurative language to tell me that you think I'm off my rocker for talking about poetry in these terms. And, look, I just did it myself. 'Off my rocker' is figurative language, too."

"All right already. You've got me tripping too. Can't we just read the poems?"

How could a teacher in her right mind refuse such a request? I reached for my copies of Nikki Giovanni's "Ego-Tripping."

> **Ego-Tripping**
> *Nikki Giovanni*
>
> *(there may be a reason why)*
> I was born in the congo
> I walked to the fertile crescent and built
>   the sphinx

I designed a pyramid so tough that a star
        that only glows every one hundred years falls
        into the center giving divine perfect light
I am bad

I sat on the throne
        drinking nectar with allah
I got hot and sent an ice age to europe
        to cool my thirst
My oldest daughter is nefertiti
        the tears from my birth pains
        created the nile
I am a beautiful woman

I gazed on the forest and burned
        out the sahara desert
        with a packet of goat's meat
and a change of clothes
I crossed it in two hours
I am a gazelle so swift
        so swift you can't catch me

        For a birthday present when he was three
I gave my son hannibal an elephant
        He gave me rome for mother's day
My strength flows ever on

My son noah built new/ark and
I stood proudly at the helm
        as we sailed on a soft summer day
I turned myself into myself and was
        jesus
        men intone my loving name
        All praises All praises
I am the one who would save

I sowed diamonds in my back yard
My bowels deliver uranium
        the filings from my fingernails are
        semi-precious jewels

> On a trip north
> I caught a cold and blew
> My nose giving oil to the arab world
> I am so hip even my errors are correct
> I sailed west to reach east and had to round off
>> the earth as I went
>> The hair from my head thinned and gold was laid
>> across three continents
>
> I am so perfect so divine so ethereal so surreal
> I cannot be comprehended
>> except by my permission
>
> I mean . . . I . . . can fly
>> like a bird in the sky . . .

Discussion

Judith Langer at the National Research Center on English Learning and Achievement at the University at SUNY-Albany, describes a master high school teacher she observed who began her class discussions with a single word: "So?" I tried this with my students after reading "Ego-Tripping."

MS. JAGO: So?

STUDENTS: "This girl has some kind of problem."
"You're the one with a problem. She's hot and she knows it."
"But who wants to be around a girl with that kind of ego? Not me."
"Maybe not you, but I do. She's playin' with you here. Something wrong that you missed that?"
"What are you talking about?"
"She knows she's exaggerating on purpose for fun. You're missing the whole thing if you don't see that. I forget the word for it. Mrs. Jago, what's it called?"

Teaching Hyperbole

On cue, I am invited to teach the class about hyperbole, intentional overstatement. What I love about this kind of lesson is that it grows out of a genuine student request. And lest you think this a one-of-a-kind experience, let me assure you that I have shown "Ego-Tripping" to more groups of students than I would readily admit to having taught, and every one included a student who quickly saw the point of Giovanni's exaggeration. Accessibility is one of the particular joys of teaching Nikki Giovanni's poetry. Kids "get" it.

I ask students to identify examples of hyperbole in the poem and, if they feel so inclined, to illustrate them. We soon have a bulletin board full of examples of this formal literary term whose meaning—I hope—will stay with students long past their sojourn in this class. And even if they forget the term, the sense of it will stay with them. It is not the technical name that matters but the sensitivity to what language can do to us as readers. This is the point of teaching children literary terminology.

My analogy may not make sense if you have never seen beachcombers roaming the shore in earphones and carrying something that looks like a watering rod, searching the sand for lost jewelry and change. It is a common sight around the Santa Monica Pier. I tell students that they don't want to become this kind of a reader, one who sifts a poem in search of literary terms. BEEEP! Found a simile! BEEEP! Three metaphors! BEEEP! Litotes, at last!

Literary terms help readers to talk about what they see and feel in a text. They help us express in shorthand what we want to communicate to others about a poem or passage. Terminology has not been invented to give the College Board items for the Advanced Placement Literature exam but to help us be more articulate about what we see and feel when we read. Good readers learn to pay close attention to every word of a poem, but they don't mistake the identification of a literary device for their goal. The goal is a powerful experience of the poem.

Ask students to apply what they have learned about *hyperbole* to this next Nikki Giovanni poem.

Communication
Nikki Giovanni

if music is the most universal language
just think of me as one whole note

if science has the most perfect language
picture me as MC^2

since mathematics can speak to the infinite
imagine me as 1 to the first power

what I mean is   one day
i'm gonna grab your love
and you'll be
satisfied

Just for fun, ask students to write their own stanza to insert inside this poem. Their assignment is to describe themselves using hyperbole. You can simply ask students to fill in the blanks:

if _____ is the _____
then think of me as _____

Teaching Connotation and Denotation

Nikki Giovanni's poem "I'm Not Lonely" resonates powerfully for teenagers, particularly girls. Familiar with the experience of falling in and out of love and having boys fall in and out of love with them, young readers know how it feels to pretend that what has happened doesn't really matter. Begin by asking students what they think might have occurred that inspired Nikki Giovanni to write this poem.

I'm Not Lonely
Nikki Giovanni

i'm not lonely
sleeping all alone

you think i'm scared
but i'm a big girl
i don't cry
or anything

i have a great
big bed
to roll around
in and lots of space
and i don't dream
bad dreams
like i used
to have that you
were leaving me
anymore

now that you're gone
i don't dream
and no matter
what you think
i'm not lonely
sleeping
all alone

You could also ask your students these questions:

- How old do you think the speaker in this poem is? Why does this make a difference?
- Who do you envision the "you" in the poem to be?
- Why do you think the speaker says she is a "big girl?" What might this suggest about how she is feeling?
- What do you infer from the line "no matter what you think"?
- Have you ever felt something like this?

"I'm Not Lonely" is a wonderful vehicle for teaching students about *denotation* and *connotation* by drawing their attention to Nikki Giovanni's artful use of the words "alone" and "lonely." The denotations of words refer to their explicit meaning as identified in a dictionary. According to the *Oxford American Dictionary*, both "alone" and "lonely" describe the state of being without companions. Connotation refers to the associations and attitudes a word calls up in the mind of a careful reader. Connotations are elusive because they comprise the various shades of suggestion and association that a word can carry. The connotations of "alone" and "lonely" differ dramatically. It is possible to be alone and quite happy. (Witness the number of times we cry out for relief, "Leave me alone!") Lonely, on the other hand, implies sadness and regret over the absence of friends or companions.

Have students reread "I'm Not Lonely" considering the connotations of "alone" and "lonely." Do they believe the speaker when she says she is not lonely or scared? Do they believe her when she says that she doesn't "cry / or anything?"

Writing to Understand

Put students in pairs and ask one partner to imagine he or she is a good friend of the speaker in the poem "I'm Not Lonely." The other partner should imagine that he or she is the speaker who has just called this friend on the phone. It's late but clearly the speaker needs to talk. Have students take out one piece of paper between them and pass it back and forth in a silent telephone conversation. If students have trouble getting started, have them reread the poem and then use one of the speaker's lines as an opening gambit. The friend may choose to console, to chide, to urge forbearance, whatever feels appropriate. In order to encourage students to develop their ideas about the speaker in the poem, require that they exchange the paper at least ten times. (Obviously such requirements are arbitrary, but I find that often students find them reassuring as though my strict guidelines were proof that this really is an important task.) When they have finished, ask if any of the pairs would like to share what they had written aloud to the class.

As a final journal entry for the day or homework assignment, have students write about the difference between "lonely" and "alone." Suggest that students refer to examples from their own experience to illustrate their explanations.

Teaching Metaphor

A poet reaches for a metaphor to make a comparison between two seemingly unrelated things for the purpose of illuminating both. A simile is a metaphor that uses "like" or "as" to make the comparison. Both metaphor and simile may be straightforward and simple or deeply and elaborately complex. In "Photography," Nikki Giovanni compares an eye with a camera, film with the heart, and God with a photo assistant.

Before they read the poem, ask students to contribute to a list of metaphors for the word "eye." What is an eye like? My students compared an eye with:

- a window
- a magnet
- a sword
- a mirror
- a black hole
- a well
- a flower
- a star

I accept all responses, though when one puzzles me, I always ask the student to explain. It is important not to let a brainstorming session become silly with random responses, but I must confess that I am often stunned by the insight a surprising image reveals.

Ask students to think about how these metaphors reveal the complex associations a poet can attach to the commonplace word "eye." Why might then a poet reach for a metaphor? What can metaphors do that simple description cannot? Have students consider what someone might be thinking by comparing an eye with a camera. Then read Nikki Giovanni's poem.

Photography
Nikki Giovanni

the eye we are told
is a camera
but the film is the heart
not the brain
and our hands joining
those that reach
develop the product

it's easy sitting in the sun
to forget that cold exists
let alone envelops

the lives of people
it's easy sitting in the sun
to forget the ice and ravages
of winter yet
there are those who would have
no other season
it's always easy when thinking
we have the best to assume
others covet it
yet surf or sea each has
its lovers and its meaning
for love

watching the red sun bleed
into the ocean
one thinks of the beauty that fire brings
if the eye is a camera and the film is the heart
then the photo assistant is god

Before beginning to discuss this poem, ask students to write for ten minutes freely, without an end in sight, simply exploring an image or idea that the poem stirred inside their heads. What I like about having students write before we begin discussing a poem is that it allows me to call on a student who may be reluctant to volunteer but who I can see from the intensity with which he or she wrote clearly has something to say. I tell students that they need not read what they have written but simply share their thinking.

TANISHA: Well, I'm not sure what Giovanni means, but I like it when she says that the film is the heart, not the brain. I know in science they teach us about light waves coming in through the eyes and going to the brain, but I think she is saying that she remembers what she sees in her heart.

Ross: What do you mean she remembers with her heart? That doesn't make sense.

Tanisha: Well, not exactly remember but maybe store the image like the one in the last stanza where she talks about a sunset. That really beautiful sunset over the ocean got her started thinking about how easy it is to forget bad times when things are going good for you. I don't get the part about God being the photo assistant, though.

Maryam: This probably isn't it but I was thinking that since God makes the sun set, maybe Giovanni calls him the photo assistant because in the same way that a photo assistant takes the exposed film and develops it, God takes her heart and develops it.

Ross: Develops it?

Maryam: Yeh, like what Tanisha was saying, the sunset makes her think about deep stuff like that some people are always cold. Giovanni is sitting there enjoying a great ocean view but something touches her heart so she starts thinking about what it would be like without the sun.

Ms. Jago: What about the line "it's easy sitting in the sun / to forget the ice and ravages / of winter"?

Ross: Maybe she is saying how even though today might be great, bad times like winter have come before are surely gonna come again.

Tanisha: And that while the eye only takes a picture of the pretty sunset today, the heart remembers the winter. See, that's what I mean about the heart remembering, Ross.

Ms. Jago: What else?

Erin: I think the title is cool. I mean you would think that a poem called "Photography" would be about real cameras or pictures, but Giovanni was using one of those metaphor things.

In *Rules for the Dance: A Handbook for Writing and Reading Metrical Verse,* poet Mary Oliver writes that "Figurative language uses figures—that is, images, 'pictures' for things—to provide clarification and intensity of thought. For grace, for illumination, for comparison, to create a language that is vibrant not only with ideas but also with the things of the world that we know through our sense experience" (1998, 67). I love the way teenagers are able to reduce our erudite explanations to "one of those metaphor things."

Teaching Repetition

Poets use repetition for emphasis. It can be used to line up similar images or to confront like with unlike. Repetition also creates sound patterns that please the ear. In "Revolutionary Dreams," Nikki Giovanni repeats the phrase "i used to dream . . ." in lines 1 and 6 suggesting that the ideas following the phrase are connected in some important way to one another. The repetition of the word "natural" at the end of lines 12, 13, and 15 emphasizes the importance of that idea within the poem and at the same time creates an insistent pattern of sound.

Ask students to reread "Photography," thinking about the effect that Giovanni's repetition of the phrase "it's easy" has upon the poem and upon them as readers.

Sometimes a poet purposely repeats a line with slight variations. Look at what Giovanni has done in "The Beep Beep Poem."

My students find this poem irresistible.

The Beep Beep Poem
Nikki Giovanni

i should write a poem
but there's almost nothing
that hasn't been said
and said and said
beautifully, ugly, blandly
excitingly
    stay in school
    make love not war
    death to all tyrants
    where have all the flowers gone
and don't they understand at kent state
the troopers will shoot . . . again

i could write a poem
i because i love walking
in the rain
and the solace of my naked
body in a tub of warm water
cleanliness may not be next
to godliness but it sure feels
good

i wrote a poem
for my father but it was so constant
i burned it up
he hates change
and i'm baffled by sameness

i composed a ditty
about encore american and worldwide news
but the editorial board
said no one would understand it
as if people have to be tricked

into sensitivity
though of course they do

i love to drive my car
hours on end
along back country roads
i love to stop for cider and apples and acorn squash
three for a dollar
i love my CB when the truckers talk
and the hum of the diesel in my ear
i love the aloneness of the road
when I ascend descending curves
the power within my toe delights me
and i fling my spirit down the highway
i love the way i feel
when i pass the moon and i holler to the stars
i'm coming through

Beep Beep

Students quickly recognize the repetition in the final stanza of "i love . . ." but often overlook the variations of the first line of the poem that begin the second, third, and fourth stanzas: "i should write a poem," "i could write a poem," "i wrote a poem," "i composed a ditty." Talk about how this parallel structure affects our reading of the poem.

While the sixties references to the shootings by the National Guard of students at Kent State University and the "where have all the flowers gone" reference may elude young readers, Giovanni's description of driving in her car at night has timeless appeal for teenagers. On the board brainstorm a list of all the things they love to do in a car (that can be shared in polite, classroom company of course).

Reread the last stanza of "The Beep Beep Poem." What makes Giovanni's description so powerful? How has she recreated her experience for readers? What do you see in your mind's eye when you read "i ascend descending curves"? How do you feel when she says "i fling my spirit down the highway"? Have you ever felt this way?

If you have students whose native language is other than English in your class, it is interesting to ask them how they might translate the last two words of this poem, "Beep Beep." What their responses can lead to is a discussion of the difficulties of translation and the liberties that a translator must often take with a poet's words in order to convey the poet's intention.

Giovanni on Figurative Language

In her essay "Meatloaf: A View of Poetry" from the collection *Racism 101,* Nikki Giovanni explains her approach to teaching poetry.

> Poetry, to me, is the association of disassociated ideas. I like clear simple images, clear simple metaphors, making clear simple statements about not-so-clear, not-so-simple human beings. In other words, I believe poets like Robert Frost are apt to be highly underrated. I want my students to tell me a story poetically. I am not especially interested in their love lives, they have lust lives and stressful social lives, but they are far too young to know, let alone knowledgeably talk about, love. I have seldom read an interesting poem about the discovery of raindrops, or clouds floating by, or sunsets either, so we eliminate these categories (1994, 175).

Giovanni goes on to describe the difficulty many of her students have writing poetry because they think that if they "put the right metaphors in the right place with the right number of syllables to a line, they will have a poem. I don't think so. I believe if they put enough passion into a real subject, they may stumble onto a poem" (1994, 167). She closes the essay with the example of meatloaf as the subject for a poem.

> I believe their responsibility as writers is to have as much sympathy for the rich as for the poor; as much pity for the beautiful as for the ugly; as much interest in the mundane as in the exotic. Meatloaf is a wonderful thing as worthy of a poem as any spring day or heroic deed. The exercise I try to instill is: Look; allow yourself to look beyond what *is*, into what *can be,* and more, into what *should be.* Poems are dreams. Dream. But dreams are conceived in reality. Meatloaf is real. Write that poem.

Nikki Giovanni uses repetition in this essay—"as much sympathy for the rich as for the poor; as much pity for the beautiful as for the ugly; as much interest in the mundane as in the exotic"—in the same way she has used repetition in her poetry, for emphasis and rhythmic pleasure. This is a writer in full command of her tools.

Like the speaker in "The Beep Beep Poem," my students often get frustrated when they sit down to write by what they think is suitable subject matter for a poem. They, too, feel that "there's almost nothing / that hasn't been said / and said and said." Well, there probably isn't if they choose for their subject matter a snowy evening or field of daffodils. But what Giovanni recommends and I heartily support is a less elevated starting point. Students know first-hand what it feels like to drive down a deserted road at night. Begin with that feeling and see where the poem leads. The metaphors will follow.

3 Writing from Models

Walking in a writer's shoes helps students learn about poetry from the inside out. Unsure about how meter works? Imitate a line from Shakespeare, inserting words of your own in place of the bard's but following his rhythmic pattern. "The quality of mercy is not strain'd;/ It droppeth as the gentle rain from heaven / Upon the place beneath." (*Merchant of Venice*, Act IV, Scene 1) Now use these lines to describe the quality of another virtue or vice. "The quality of ardor is not cold; / It burneth as the coals of hell / Inside a lover's heart." Some students are adept at counting beats and marking accents, but others will find imitation a more powerful way to understand how rhythm works.

I struggled for years trying to explain epic similes until I stumbled upon the idea of having students borrow one of Homer's and tailor it to their own purposes:

> "As a hundred-year-old man stabs with withered fingers that bear the fork for a remaining pea on his plate, so did heavy-eyed, soccer-sore Brian pick at his godly Corn Flakes" (Brian Ziff)

> "As a mouse scurries back to its hole, chased by a cat, and fearful for its life, so did Manisha scramble about her messy room, gathering her papers for school." (Manisha Parekh)

Modeling their own lines after Homer's, students internalize both the structure and the point of epic similes.

Nikki Giovanni has written a number of poems ripe for use as models. Many follow no formal rhyme or rhythm pattern but achieve an internal structure that feels natural to student writers. Along with what students learn about informal form from imitating Nikki Giovanni's poetry, it also helps them avoid the four most egregious errors common to teenage poetry:

- Adjectivitis: the layering of adjectives instead of careful choice of powerful verbs and nouns

- Clichés: tired, worn expressions that 15-year-olds think are fresh and new like "still waters run deep" or "my one and only love"

- Forced rhyme: rhyme that runs counter to sense causing a writer to say almost anything to complete a line

- Multi-syllabic words like "commitment," "relationship," "generosity," "meaningful," and "apprehension"

What makes rooting out these errors from student poetry so difficult is the fact that teenagers most often use them in a line that is utterly heartfelt. How can I tell a timid tenth grader who is pouring out her guts on the page that "our throbbing hearts became as one in full commitment / and the relationship more meaningful with every passing moment of time" needs revision? I prefer to teach through example. The following poem of Giovanni's employs one adjective, "pleasant," no clichés, no rhyme, and no word over two syllables. And it is a marvelous, complex poem.

The World Is Not a Pleasant Place to Be
Nikki Giovanni

the world is not a pleasant place
to be without

someone to hold and be held by

a river would stop
its flow if only
a stream were there
to receive it

an ocean would never laugh
if clouds weren't there
to kiss her tears

the world is not
a pleasant place to be without
someone

After reading the poem aloud, I ask students to reread it to themselves and to think about its structure. What is happening in the first and last stanzas? What purpose do the middle two stanzas serve? Students are quick to recognize that the middle stanzas are metaphors for how the speaker in the poem feels about being alone. They offer concrete examples of how "the world is not a pleasant place / to be without / someone." We talk about why Giovanni might have chosen to develop her idea in this way. What do the metaphors achieve that more explanation could not? Again, students see immediately how the images of the river and the ocean give readers a concrete example of the feeling Giovanni is trying to convey about being without someone to love.

Creating a Class Poem

For the next step in learning through example, I tell students that we are going to borrow Nikki Giovanni's first and last stanzas for a class poem of our own. Their task is to create a metaphor similar to the ones Giovanni has used to demonstrate the big idea that "the world is not a pleasant place / to be without / someone." For those who have difficulty getting started, I suggest they choose an object and then write the name of this object followed by "would never . . ." This is usually enough direction to get the most reluctant writer going. Students are encouraged by the idea that they only have to write three short lines.

As a prop, I hand out 3" X 5" index cards and ask students to recopy their stanzas neatly on the card. Those who finish first begin to sort what their classmates have written, looking for a natural order for their poem. I put one student on a computer and have him or her begin typing. What I particularly like about this part of the assignment is that when there is an indecipherable (or unintelligible) word in a poem, the student editors can easily check with the writer. An enormous amount of natural revising goes on with relatively little input from me. Instead of typing in full names which seem to distract from the brief lines, students came up with the idea of simply listing initials at the end of each stanza.

The World Is Not a Pleasant Place

inspired by and dedicated to Nikki Giovanni
by Mrs. Jago's Period 1 English class

the world is not a pleasant place
to be without
someone to hold and be held by

a stage would never be lit
without an actor
to grace its floors

—S. C.

what clock would tick
without time to guide it?

—F. N.

a sun would never shine
if there were no eyes to see it

—K. P.

a student would never fail
if there were no tests to judge him

—M. G.

a star cannot fly
without wings

—E. B.

a hope would never surface
without the help
of angels' shoulders

—A. G.

M & Ms would melt in your hand
if your mouth wasn't there
to eat them

—C. W.

a comedian
would not be funny
without your smile

—T. G.

my lips would not taste so sweet
if yours weren't there to kiss them

—D. G.

a mother would not be complete
without her children

—A. M.

the world is not
a pleasant place to be without
someone

Overnight I make copies of the class poem and in the morning we perform for an audience of ourselves—a readers theater reading of their poem. I then ask students to choose a stanza—not their own—that struck them for its poignancy and write about what they think the creator of this image was feeling and thinking. I then give these readers' responses to the appropriate author. It doesn't worry me that some writers receive many responses and others none. The truth is that certain stanzas are more evocative than others. Without having to assign A's, B's, or C's; students have received critical feedback on what they wrote. Inevitably, the stanzas that students identify as most powerful are those which avoid adjectivitis, clichés, pointless rhyme, and multisyllabic words.

Finally, we talk about what imitating Nikki Giovanni's poem taught them about the use of metaphors. What do they now understand about "The World Is Not a Pleasant Place" that they didn't before?

Using a Model

Sometimes I come across a poem that I am certain students will love imitating. "I Wrote a Good Omelet" was one such find. What I have to be careful about as I set the assignment, though, is to offer the Giovanni poem as a model rather than a straightjacket.

I Wrote a Good Omelet
Nikki Giovanni

I wrote a good omelet . . . and ate a hot poem . . .
after loving you

Buttoned my car . . . and drove my coat home . . . in the
rain . . .
after loving you

I goed on red . . . and stopped on green . . . floating
somewhere in between
being here and being there . . .
after loving you

I rolled my bed . . . turned down my hair . . . slightly
confused but . . . I don't care . . .
Laid out my teeth . . . and gargled my gown. . . then I stood
. . . and laid me down. . .

to sleep. . .
after loving you

As we did with "The World Is Not a Pleasant Place," we begin
by discussing the poem. There is no point in having students use
a poem as a model if they have no idea what the poem itself is
doing.

Ms. Jago: So, what do you make of this poem?

Alexi: This guy is really messed up.

Janet: It's not a guy. Guys don't roll their hair or put on a gown.

Alexi: O.K., it's a girl but her head's turned inside out over what
just happened with this guy she likes.

Deana: Yeh, she's totally confused and can't even talk straight. I
know how that feels. It's like when something really great
happens and you're almost in shock.

Janet: What I like is the way she seems totally happy about
being confused, like she's enjoying the mental chaos.

Ms. Jago: I love the title. How could you resist reading a poem with "omelet" in the title?

Alexi: Yeh, imagine if the writer called it "Being in Love," or "A Night to Remember."

Deana: Boring.

Ms. Jago: So what makes this poem not boring?

Janet: It's what you always say about show don't tell. The lady in the poem doesn't tell the reader anything about how she is feeling. She just shows us how her mind has been totally jumbled.

Alexi: Like she was in a blender or something.

Ms. Jago: Well, that's what I'd like you to try to recreate in a poem of your own. Think about something that has had this kind of effect upon you. It could be something good like a kiss or something bad like a car accident. Find a phrase to describe what happened and repeat this line in your poem the way Nikki Giovanni did with "after loving you." Then I'd like you to imitate the way she has portrayed a mind that's more than a bit mixed up. It's up to you whether you adopt a tone similar to her light-hearted one or find that your subject matter takes you in another direction. See what happens. No one may leave class without handing me a poem (I find such dramatic and dictatorial orders sometimes help to get students moving. Of course I allow anyone who asks to work more on the poem at home to do so.)

Some students borrowed heavily from Giovanni's original:

I Ate an Old Song

I sang a sad sandwich . . . and ate an old song . . .
after leaving you

Packed up my plane . . . and sat in my bag . . .
        in my pain . . .
after leaving you

I combed my teeth . . . and flossed my hair . . .
        slightly confused . . . but I don't care. . .
Laid out my work . . . and finished my bed . . .
        then I thought . . . and laid my head . . .

to sleep . . .
after missing you
                                    —*Edward Brodsky*

When I Heard about Patty

I went up my bed
And laid on my stair
After hearing about Patty

Screams came out of my eyes
And tears out of my mouth
After hearing about Patty

Sadness was in my head
And hate in my heart
After hearing about Patty

I hung up your message
And erased the phone
After hearing about Patty
                        —*Claudia Mendez*

Other students took interesting liberties with the form:

I Wrote a Nice Sweater

I wrote a nice sweater
And wore an old poem
After seeing you

I brushed my breakfast
And ate my teeth
After seeing you.

I put on my car
And drove my suit
After seeing you

I took a car wash
I went on a break
SNAP OUT OF IT!

I got in my job
I lost an accident
Damn, I'm lost without you.
—*Chris Hruby*

Still others abandoned the form altogether though they clearly still imitated Giovanni's description of mental confusion:

Where Am I?   .

wake up at half past hung-over, realize I'm in the wrong bed
        jeez. what a night.
check my ID to remember my name, realize I'm in the wrong house
crawl outside to drive on home, realize I'm in the wrong neighborhood
        jeez. what a night.
get lost finding the freeway, realize I'm in the wrong city
check my glove compartment for a map, realize I'm in the wrong car
        jeez. what a night.
get home at half past dark, realize it's the wrong day

check the messages, realize it was the wrong party
    but jeez. what a night.
—Charles Matzner

And then there is the student who takes the idea and runs in an altogether different direction.

I woke up with my mords wixed.

I bot out of ged

Dalked woundstairs and said, "Mey Hom."
I ded the fog and baked my wother up.
My fore whamily was looking at me like I cas wazy.
I said, "I woke up with my mords wixed."

I scheft for lool
Faw my sriends
They looked at me like I cas wazy
I said. "I woke up with my mords wixed."
I dent the spay alone.

When I hot gome
De thockter was there
He mopened my outh
Thuck stings in my ears
And then asked te to malk
I said, "I woke up with my mords wixed."
He said, "Well nats thot soo terious."
The doctor's tace furned red
And he walked out hy mouse
And I looked at py marents
And they said, "I guess it cas wontageous."
—Alexi Glickman

Without doubt Alexi's poem was influenced by the book he had been reading before class—Russell Hoban's *Ridley Walker.* In this novel, Hoban creates a language of his own which readers must figure out as they go along. For the full impact of Alexi's poem, try reading it out loud.

Alexi read his poem to the class from his seat at one of the computers. It was still hot and the other students felt this. Suddenly everyone wanted to share what they had written. Now any teacher who has stood in front of a blackboard as long as I have knows that this is a very good sign that the lesson has gone well. Students loved what they had created and thoroughly enjoyed the invitation to be wacky. Some read aloud stream-of-consciousness pieces that made no sense whatever to me as I listened but did contain some remarkably stark and interesting images: "Apricots never sleep," "Because the periodic table is coming for me," "I love the feel of brown carpet on my wall, even if I can't reach the lock." (Occasionally I worry that if our society did have a Thought Police, I would most surely end up doing time for corrupting our youth.)

When students returned the next day, we read Nikki Giovanni's poem "I Wrote a Good Omelet" one more time. I asked students to count the adjectives (There are two: "good" and "hot"). I asked them to look for multi-syllabic words. (Unless you count "omelet" and "borrowed" as 3-syllable words—which I don't— there are none.) We talked about how the simplicity of Giovanni's language strengthened her poem. I pointed out to them how without really trying they had imitated this feature of her style in their poems, omitting the usual flowery adjectives and instead focusing on powerful nouns and verbs. We looked at the two rhymes in the poem ("I goed on red . . . and stopped on green . . . floating / somewhere in between" and "I rolled my bed . . . turned down my hair . . . slightly / confused . . . but I don't care . . .") and talked about how Giovanni's intermittent use of rhyme was more effective than a forced rhyme of "home" with, for example, "moan."

I always try to make an assignment like this one on modeling serve multiple purposes. On one level, I want students to have opportunities for creating original work. I worry that formal English classes abandon creative writing in order to focus on analytical writing. At the same time I believe that this kind of writing can be a vehicle to deep understanding about literature and the magic that poetry can work upon readers. Modeling their own poems after a master's helps students experiment with forms that they might never attempt on their own. It also helps students to recognize poetic devices as they read. Creative writing, creative reading. One can be in the service of the other.

Additional Nikki Giovanni poems that work well as models

Mothers
Nikki Giovanni

the last time i was home
to see my mother we kissed
exchanged pleasantries
and unpleasantries pulled a warm
comforting silence around
us and read separate books

i remember the first time
i consciously saw her
we were living in a three room
apartment on burns avenue

mommy always sat in the dark
i don't know how i knew that but she did

that night i stumbled into the kitchen
maybe because i've always been
a night person or perhaps because i had wet
the bed
she was sitting on a chair
the room was bathed in moonlight diffused through
         tiny window panes
she may have been smoking but maybe not
her hair was three-quarters her height
which made me a strong believer in the samson myth
and very black

i'm sure i just hung there by the door
i remember thinking: what a beautiful lady

she was very deliberately waiting
perhaps for my father to come home
from his night job or maybe for a dream
that had promised to come by
"come here" she said "i'll teach you
a poem: *i see the moon*
                the moon sees me
                god bless the moon
                and god bless me"
i taught that to my son
 who recited it for her
just to say we must learn
to bear the pleasures
as we have borne the pains

A wonderful companion piece to teach alongside the poem "Mothers" is a short story by Jerome Weidman called "My Father Sits in the Dark." This is how it begins:

My father has a peculiar habit. He is fond of sitting in the dark, alone. Sometimes I come home very late. The house is dark. I let myself in quietly because I do not want to disturb my mother.

She is a light sleeper. I tiptoe into my room and undress in the dark. I go to the kitchen for a drink of water. My bare feet make no noise. I step into the room and almost trip over my father. He is sitting in a kitchen chair, in his pajamas, smoking his pipe.

"Hello, Pop." I say.

"Hello, son."

"Mothers" can be used as a model for students to write about an important adult in their lives and an occasion when they had special quiet time with him or her.

Kidnap Poem
Nikki Giovanni

ever been kidnapped
by a poet
if i were a poet
i'd kidnap you
put you in my phrases and meter
you to jones beach
or maybe coney island
or maybe just to my house
lyric you in lilacs
dash you in the rain
blend into the beach
to complement my see
play the lyre for you
ode you with my love song
anything to win you
wrap you in the red Black green
show you off to mama
yeah if i were a poet i'd kid
nap you

After reading "Kidnap Poem," ask students to brainstorm other occupations: banker, painter, nurse, pitcher, lawyer, teacher, gardener. Then have students choose one and imagine what this person might do to keep someone he or she loves close.

Winter
Nikki Giovanni

Frogs burrow the mud
snails bury themselves
and I air my quilts
preparing for the cold

Dogs grow more hair
mothers make oatmeal
and little boys and girls
take Father John's Medicine

Bears store fat
chipmunks gather nuts
and I collect books
For the coming winter

"Winter" is a natural model for a class poem. Have each student write a stanza and compile them into one long collaborative poem. For variety, change the season.

4 Taking a Critical Stance

■ ■

Reading what others have said about a writer's work can help students refine and even reconsider their own responses. What follows are excerpts from critical reviews of Nikki Giovanni's poetry as well as Giovanni's own reflections on writing. No attempt has been made here to present an homogenized view. Instead these essays are offered as thoughtful interpretations open to discussion.

Readings

Nikki Giovanni

In this essay from *Racism 101,* Giovanni uses the metaphor of gardening to explore the issues of how and why writers write. Is it to be remembered? Or is it to do the work that they were born to do?

I Plant Geraniums

I plant geraniums each spring. It's not that I am a geranium lover or even a plant lover; it's just that at spring there should be an acknowledgment of something new, some rebirth, some faith in constant change. I don't particularly like grubs or Japanese beetles; I actually hate flying things. My allergies allow me to plant my tomatoes but not to harvest them. Something about the fuzz that were I willing and able to pay six hundred dollars, my dermatologist could explain exactly why I break out when I touch it. I actually don't care. I'm quite content, in fact, to press family and friends into tomato-picking service: "It's my allergies, you know."

I'm not a critic, though I have been known to write a book review or two. When younger, I actually thought my opinion counted. I have since learned. When younger, I thought one of the particulars of being "Homo sapiens" was to communicate. I have not learned not to, though I am cautious when I try. Life is far too serious to take seriously. All the important things happen without our knowledge, consent, or active, conscious participation. We are conceived. We live. We die. We have no opinion on these subjects. Most of us don't even get to name ourselves. WE can lie about our ages, but on the Gregorian or Chinese or Islamic calendar we are a certain age. That old expression, I think they call it a social lie, that "you don't look it or would never have thought you are . . ." takes away one of the crowning achievements of humans . . . that you survived. Of course, some people commit suicide to control the time of their deaths, but the end result is the same. Granting all that, which is, after all, not so much to grant, I support the concept of human life.

Shakespeare is lucky. There is an old African saying: "You are not dead until you are forgotten." Many groups share that belief, including some American Indians. The Euro-American must believe it because he works so hard to keep his history alive. It's fine by me. I hope, like Shakespeare, to one day be a *Jeopardy!* Subject. I hope high school seniors quake at the fact that they have to take Giovanni before they graduate. I certainly can see the controversy over who actually wrote my poems; why did I never receive a "major" poetry award? These things get many a professor tenured, keeping many a family fed. One might even win promotion to "full" professor with the lucky and unusual discovery of some obscure grocery list proving once and for all, until deconstruction, that I do have false teeth. These things matter.

But I don't think Shakespeare had to worry about it. I think he had to write plays telling the king, "You are a fool" while keeping his head upon his shoulders. He had to tell the people who scrimped and saved to see his productions, "You are jealous, small-minded idiots who will kill the one you love: He had to show his public that the savage was more noble than their pretentious societies while making them come back. He had to expose literal-mindedness for the foolishness that it is. Shakespeare was a working artist.

How could he have known that five or six hundred years later he would be required reading? Should he have foreseen this possibility and tempered his judgments to match? Should not he have considered the possibility that his words would be difficult to read, and should he therefore have anticipated modern usage: Shouldn't we hold him to the same standards as the Constitution and Bible and bring him "up to date"? I think not. I think we should leave him in the brilliance of his expression. We need, we modern artists and critics, to do exactly what Shakespeare did. Write for now. Think for now. Express ourselves in our best possible vernacular for now. Will we be remembered? I doubt it. Most people are not remembered. And most people who would remember the people are not remembered. We have no true concept of what "Homo sapiens" has forgotten, though surely some of it was good and some of it was useless.

Shelley or Keats, I always mess up which one, talked about tending his own garden. Or was it Voltaire? I plant geraniums. No one will remember that. I have an allergy to tomato fuzz. No one will care. I write poetry and sometimes prose. No one will know me . . . let alone what I thought I did. But while I live, during this all too brief period between birth and death, my life and work have been meaningful to me. "The rest is silence."

Source: Nikki Giovanni, "I Plant Geraniums," *Racism 101,* William Morrow and Company, Inc., New York, 1994, pp. 27–29. Reprinted with permission.

Virginia Fowler

In the foreword to *Racism 101,* the scholar Virginia Fowler introduces readers who may or may not be familiar with Nikki Giovanni's poetry to her manner of working in prose.

Foreword

"A real writer," James Baldwin says in "Alas, Poor Richard," "is always shifting and changing and searching," a fact that often creates an "intensity of . . . bewilderment" in the writer's audience. But despite this inconvenience to readers, reviewers, and critics, "a real writer" will indeed challenge attempts to pigeonhole her or his work because, Baldwin continues, that "work is fatally entangled with his personal fortunes and misfortunes, his personality, and the social facts and attitudes of his time."

Baldwin's observations have particular relevance to this most recent collection of essays by Nikki Giovanni, "a real writer" by anyone's definition. The essays brought together here span the past five years of the poet's life; they project her view of the world that her new perspective as a faculty member in a large research university affords her. Readers familiar with Giovanni's earlier life and work—both poetry and prose—will not perhaps be surprised by many of her reactions to being a member of one of society's most conservative institutions, though they will perhaps find it remarkable that this most iconoclastic and individualistic writer made a decision to accept a position in *any* institution. That the perspective afforded by this decision should find its initial expression in prose rather than poetry is hardly surprising; what *will,* perhaps, startle the reader of this collection is the decidedly poetic sensibility Giovanni brings to the many unpoetic subjects she addresses here. Emily Dickinson's famous dictum that the poet should "tell all the Truth but tell it slant" is certainly true of many of these essays, which work indirectly and figuratively to delineate "the truth" about education, educational institutions, racism, writing, and a host of other subjects.

The prophetic and truth-telling qualities that we associate with the poetry that came out of the Black Arts Movement of the sixties and early seventies are as much in evidence in these essays as they were in Giovanni's earliest and most "militant" poetry. But the changes wrought in American culture by the last twenty-five years are quite evident in the modulations of the voice that speaks from these pages. What is constant in Nikki Giovanni, from her first book of poems to this most recent collection, are the fundamental

values that shape her vision of society, culture, and life it-
self: a belief in the necessity to fight injustice wherever it
appears and in whatever form; a commitment to an histori-
cal perspective, to looking at the present with a fully in-
formed sense of the past; a respect, often even a reverence,
for the past and present struggles of African-American
people; a desire to find underlying connections between and
among people and events; and, of course, an abiding belief
in the integrity and the power of the individual. Whether
she is speculating about space exploration, indicting higher
education for the inequities it perpetuates and its frequent
failure to accomplish its mission, or offering her own ver-
sion of a film about Malcolm X, these values inform her
attempt to get at the fundamental core of the subject, the
heart of the matter.

In form, most of these essays are like jazz compositions,
relying on highly individualized improvisation to develop
their themes. To reduce those themes to their essence is to
miss altogether the meaning and significance of the essays,
for Giovanni's *improvisatory performance* of her themes is what
ultimately matters. It is also what constitutes the *art* of these
essays. They are not the sort of academic essays we would
normally expect to read on the subjects addressed here. No,
these pieces are artistic expressions of a particular way of
looking at the world, featuring a performing voice capable
of dizzying displays of virtuosity. Like a jazz musician, she
is both composer and performer, and the prose style she
has created is as distinctive as a Charlie Parker's or a Nina
Simone's.

Louis Armstrong once said that if you have to ask what
jazz is, you'll never know. The same admonishment must

be made to readers of this volume. Those who do know, however, should sit back and listen to the music.

Source: Virginia Fowler, 1994. Foreword to *Racism 101* New York: William Morrow. pp. 5–7. Reprinted with permission.

Curt Schleier

This 1996 interview with Curt Schleier, a reporter for the *Detroit News* offers biographical insight into Nikki Giovanni's work as well as a sense of the lady behind the lines.

Versed in Protest

Nikki Giovanni is one of America's best-known poets. She's the author of more than a dozen books, winner of many awards and honorary degrees, and currently a professor of English at Virginia Polytechnic. But of course all that doesn't matter when she's waiting for a table at a restaurant. And waiting. And waiting.

Giovanni is on the phone from San Francisco where she's touring to promote her new collection, *The Selected Poems of Nikki Giovanni,* and she is angry as she tells the story: "Until I mentioned my hostess' name, the maitre d' just left me standing there."

Racism is still pervasive in this country, she maintains, and always will be "until America owns up to it." And yes, there are hills and valleys, but when it comes down to it, blacks are always left waiting for tables. "I'm happy for Whitney Houston and her success with the movie *Waiting to Exhale,*" says Giovanni. "But I'm not happy that one of the great voices of our century, Aretha Franklin, was never seriously invited to Hollywood. This is an amazing thing. Any other star who had achieved what she has achieved would have been. She was in one movie, *The Blues Brothers,* and she played a cook. This is a woman we should have been creating parts for."

Giovanni has been speaking her mind for a long time. A decade ago, she was one of the few prominent African-Americans to speak against a boycott of segregated South Africa, which led to threats on her life. "I felt it was hard to boycott a country. I caught a lot more flak than it was worth. It was a level of grief I didn't deserve."

About a year and a half ago Giovanni was diagnosed with cancer. She had half a lung and two ribs removed. "I'm as fine as anybody who's been told she has cancer can be," she says. "I feel fine now, but it's never a question of beating cancer. Even if they tell you they got it all, it's a question of living with it."

Giovanni came of age during the height of the civil rights struggle. Born in Knoxville, Tennessee, and brought up there and in Cincinnati, she attended Fisk University in Nashville, where she helped form a campus chapter of the Student Nonviolent Coordinating Committee (SNCC). It was around this time that she began to write poetry.

Much of her early work was centered on the civil rights struggle, and seems to reflect equal parts militancy, anger and an overwhelming sense of frustration. Poems such as "Detroit Conference of Unity and Art (For HRB—HRB being a militant H. Rap Brown—set at a conference she attended in 1967, reflect her understanding of history and pride at playing a role in so pivotal a time. Even in this early period, though, there was an erotic earthiness to some of her work. Poems like "Seduction" are, well hot. Other regular topics of her work include creativity, politics and her personal life. "Most poets will say the political is personal and the personal is political," she says. Whatever the subject though, there is a musical quality to her work; read her poems and hear the blues or jazz riffs. She is pleased when a reporter mentions that. "I think there is a certain rhythm to my poems. I love the blues, the music I hear in my head is gospel."

Source: Curt Schleier, 1996. "Versed in Protest." *The Detroit News.* Reprinted with permission.

Ida Lewis

The following is excerpted from the foreword to Nikki Giovanni's collection *My House,* published in 1972.

It is said that when the subject is complicated try drawing a simple picture, but even to this writer, who is both friend and sometimes editor to poet Nikki Giovanni, she cannot be simply understood or explained—she must be experienced and felt. The judgement, however, has been offered before: Nikki Giovanni is the Princess of Black Poetry.

She is adored not only because she is Black America's most celebrated word magician, but also because she is an extraordinary example of the young Black spirit enjoying a newly reopened life. She has said, "You must do what you think is important the way you think it's important, being trapped neither by the past of your people nor your future personal hopes."

It is indeed among the marvels of Nikki's art that her work has so deeply penetrated the hearts of so many. But why is that so? Is it something shocking about her poetry, something lascivious? Is it those "Revolutionary Dreams" that delight and excite the iron palate of today's readers? I've seen Nikki mobbed in Bloomingdale's department store by Black and white customers; I've walked with her down Fifth Avenue and watched a man who was saying "hi" to her walk into an oncoming taxi. She rides her bicycle to Harlem to buy books at Micheaux's and draws a crowd. She was recently the first poet to do poetry on the Tonight show with Flip Wilson. But none of this has stopped her from answering her mail: from youngsters in private schools in Vermont, "Miss Giovanni, I love you. I go to private school—am I irrelevant?"; from men in prison who advise her on how her son should be reared. "Don't forget," she writes, "Angela Davis went to private school and Malcolm X graduated from prison." Her pragmatic existential idealism forces her to take each case, each person personally.

Nikki Giovanni is a product of the thunderous and explosive sixties, endowed with a powerful and inquiring mind absorbed with the Black America of that decade—our vision of ourselves. And, like a painter's brush, her life depicts what Black America can see and feel. "Service is the key," she says over and over again. "If I can't find a way to serve and be serviced we won't make it."

Reading Nikki Giovanni is an intoxicating experience. It is certainly by no means an act of escape. Her work excites all of one's nerves. The head spins, the soul is forever invaded; one is tempted to cry out, Amen! Through the works of Nikki Giovanni one realizes that though the fire is

just beginning to burn, the flame is three hundred years
old.

Source: Ida Lewis, 1983. Foreword to *My House,* New York: William Morrow. pp. ix–xv. Reprinted with permission.

Having Students Take a Critical Stance toward the Work of Nikki Giovanni

Suggested Essay Topics

■ Assign groups of students essays from *Racism 101* to read and discuss. Essays of particular interest to high school students include: "Paper Dolls, Iron Skillets, Libraries, and Museums," "I Plant Geraniums," "Black is the Noun," "His Name Is Malcolm," "Shooting for the Moon," "Meatloaf: A View of Poetry." Then have students individually write a paper exploring their reaction to Giovanni's essay. Do they agree or disagree with what she has said here? Remind students that they must support their opinions with evidence.

■ Ask students to write an essay that explores Nikki Giovanni's use of figurative language. How has Giovanni employed metaphor, simile, personification, and other literary devices in her work? Require that students include in their essays the definitions of any literary terminology that they use and that they cite from specific poems. This assignment is excellent for teaching students how to quote poetry within the body of an essay.

■ During the sixties young people voiced loud and sometimes violent protests against the war in Vietnam and racial injustice. Have students research the student activist movement and then write about whether or not they think they would have participated in such protests. Ask them to explain why they would or why not.

■ Have students choose one of Nikki Giovanni's collections of poetry and write a review for the school newspaper of this volume. What poems would they recommend to other students? What is there about Giovanni's work that would appeal to other teenage writers? Is there anything about Giovanni's work that might repel some readers?

■ Ask students to choose a poem of Nikki Giovanni's that seems particularly autobiographical. Then have students write an account of what they think happened in the poet's life to inspire such a poem. Encourage students to speculate but not wildly. They must be able to point to some evidence in the poem to support their speculations.

■ Pair poems from Nikki Giovanni's early and late work, for example "Poem for Black Boys" (1970) with "Resignation" (1990) or "Intellectualism" (1970) with "A Journey" (1990). All of these poems and many more that would be interesting to compare can be found in the collection *The Selected Poems of Nikki Giovanni*, (1996). Have students write a comparison-and-contrast paper focusing on the ways in which Nikki Giovanni's poetry has evolved over time. What aspects of her style and content have remained constant? Which have changed?

5 Extensions and Connections

Connecting Nikki Giovanni's Poetry to Commonly-taught Pieces of Literature

One of the obstacles to introducing new work into a curriculum is figuring out what the new material will displace. Most English teachers are frustrated by how little time we have with students given the enormity and importance of what we have to teach them. (Math and history teachers may see things otherwise, but it is unlikely they will ever see this book.) An alternative to creating a new unit on Nikki Giovanni is to integrate the study of her poetry into an already established lesson plan. For example, one of the most commonly-taught high school texts is *Romeo and Juliet*.

Romeo and Juliet

Year after year Shakespeare's themes of love, misunderstanding, and "woe" resonate for teenage readers. In a volume called *Love Poems* (1997), Nikki Giovanni has collected fifty-four poems focusing on these same themes. Depending upon your students' inclinations and your own instructional goals, have students read Giovanni's poems before, during, or after their reading of the play. Have students compare the relationship that Nikki Giovanni describes in "How Do You Write a Poem" with that of Shakespeare's "star-crossed lovers."

How Do You Write a Poem?
Nikki Giovanni

how do you write a poem
about someone so close
to you that when you say ahhhhh
they say chuuuu
what can they ask you to put
on paper that isn't already written
on your face
and does the paper make it
any more real
that without them
life would be not
impossible but certainly
more difficult
and why would someone need
a poem to say when i come
home if you're not there
i search the air
for your scent
would i search any less
if i told the world
i don't care at all
and love is so complete
that touch or not we blend
to each other the things
that matter aren't all about
baaaanging (i can be baaaanged all
day long) but finding a spot
where i can be free
of all the physical
and emotional bullshit
and simply sit with a cup
of coffee and say to you
"i'm tired" don't you know
those are my love words
and say to you "how was your

day" doesn't that show
i care or say to you "we lost
a friend" and not want to share
that loss with strangers
don't you already know
what i feel and if
you don't maybe
i should check my feelings

For a particularly immature class (we have all had them), you may need to prepare readers for some of the language or references in these love poems. Of course the same kind of references exist in Shakespeare, but unless the teacher explains them literally, these go right past most students and parents. Students are unlikely to miss or misunderstand Giovanni's use of the word "bullshit."

I Take Master Card
(Charge Your Love to Me)
Nikki Giovanni

I've heard all the stories

'bout how you don't deserve me

'cause I'm so strong and beautiful and wonderful and you could

never live up to what you know I should have but I just want to
    let

you know:

I take Master Card

You can love me as much as your heart can stand

Then put the rest on

Account and pay the interest

Each month until we get this settled

You see we modern women do comprehend

That we deserve a whole lot more

Than what is normally being offered but we are trying

To get aligned with the modern world

So baby you can love me all

You like 'cause you're pre-approved

And you don't have to sign on

The bottom line

Charge it up

'til we just can't take no more

it's the modern way

I take Master Card

To see your Visa

And I deal with a Discovery but I don't want any American

Express 'cause like the Pointer Sisters say: I need a slow hand

Walt Whitman and Emily Dickinson

While it may seem obvious that Nikki Giovanni be included in the American Literature curriculum, what is also obvious is that most teachers who use a chronological approach don't get to the twentieth century until May, leaving about 15 minutes of class time for any writer after Fitzgerald and Hemingway. A natural place to slip Nikki Giovanni's poetry into the traditional sequence is in counterpoint position to Walt Whitman and Emily Dickinson. Both of these poets were considered "new voices" for their times just as Giovanni has been for hers. Compare "Song of Myself" with Giovanni's poem "Ego-Tripping" (page 18). Compare the following poem written on the death of rap singer Tupak Shakur with Dickinson's reflections on death: "I heard a fly buzz," "There's been a Death, in the Opposite House," "Grief is a Mouse," "The Whole of it came not at once."

All Eyez On U
(for 2Pac Shakur 1971–1996)
Nikki Giovanni

as I tossed and turned unable to achieve sleep unable to control anxiety unable to comprehend why

2Pac is not with us

if those who lived by the sword died by the sword there would be no
    white men on earth

if those who lived on hatred died on hatred there would be no KKK

if those who lived by lies died by lies there would be nobody on wall

street in executive suites in academic offices instructing the young don't tell me he got what he deserved   he deserved a chariot and

the accolades of a grateful people

he deserved his life

it is as clear as a mountain stream as defining as a lightning strike

as terrifying as sun to vampires

2Pac told the truth

there were those who called it dirty   gansta rap inciting

there were
those who never wanted to be   angry at conditions but angry
at the messenger who reported: *your kitchen has roaches your toilet*
is overflowing your basement has so much water the rats are in the
living room
your house is in disorder

and 2Pac told you about it

what a beautiful boy graceful carriage melodic voice sharp wit
     intellectual
breadth what a beautiful boy to lose

no me   never me   I do not believe east coast west coast
               I saw
them murder Emmett Till I saw them murder Malcolm X   I saw
them murder   Martin Luther King   I witnessed them shooting
Rap Brown I saw them beat LeRoi Jones   I saw them fill their jails
I see them burning churches   not me   never me   I do not believe
This is some sort of mouth action   this is some sort of political
action and they picked well   they picked the brightest freshest
fruit from the tallest tree   what a beautiful boy

but he will not go away   as Malcolm did not go away
          as Emmett
Till did not go away   your shooting him will not take him from us
His spirit will fill our hearts   his courage will strengthen us for the
challenge   his truth will straighten our backbones

you know, Socrates had a mother   she too watched her son drink
hemlock   she too asked why   but Socrates stood firm and would
not lie to save himself   2Pac has a mother   the lovely Afeni had
to bury her son   it is not right

it is not right that this young warrior is cut down   it is not right for
the old to bury the young   it is not right

this generation mourns 2Pac as my generation mourned Till as we
all mourn Malcolm   this wonderful young warrior

Sonia Sanchez said when she learned of his passing she walked all day
walking the beautiful warrior home to our ancestors I just cried as all
mothers cry for the beautiful boy who said he and Mike Tyson would
never be allowed to be free at the same time who told the truth about
them and who told the truth about us who is our beautiful warrior

there are those who wanted to make *him* the problem
          who wanted
to believe if they silenced 2Pac all would be quiet on the ghetto
front there are those who testified that the problem wasn't the
          conditions
but the people talking about them

they took away band   so the boys started scratching they took away
gym   so the boys started break dancing the boys started rapping
cause they gave them the guns and the drugs but not the schools an
libraries

what a beautiful boy to lose

and we mourn 2Pac Shakur and we reach out to his mother and we
hug ourselves in sadness and shame

and we are compelled to ask:
R U Happy, Mz Tucker? 2Pac is gone
R U Happy?

Another evocative American Literature pairing is that of Nikki
Giovanni's poem "Revolutionary Dreams" (page 16) with Denise
Levertov's poem "At the Justice Department, November 15, 1969."
Denise Levertov was an antiwar activist and Nikki Giovanni is
committed to black revolution. Have students compare and con-
trast the two poems for attitudes towards creating change in soci-
ety.

Connecting Nikki Giovanni's Poetry to Other Disciplines

The Social Studies Connection
Though it may seem difficult for many of us to believe, the sixties
is now being taught as a historical period. If you are part of an
American Literature/American History team or simply would like
to bring a literary perspective to the events students are learning
about the sixties, Nikki Giovanni's early poetry offers a unique
insight into the militant attitude of the civil rights movement and
Black Art, with strong emphasis on the female experience. There
is much in these early poems that will disturb young readers, but
that is one of the reasons they are so powerful. The poems are
cultural artifacts of the times. Nikki Giovanni's collection of es-
says, *Racism 101,* includes a short piece called "The Sixties." It
begins, "My personal problem with what is called 'the sixties,'
roughly the period between the Brown decision of the Supreme
Court (1954) and the election of Richard Nixon (1968), is that I

think we won"(1994, 35). The essay concludes with this obser-
vation:

> Nothing in the sixties takes away the problems of the seven-
> ties, eighties, or nineties, or alleviates the pain of the post-World
> War II era. The sixties, however, solved the problems of the
> sixties—overt and lawful segregation; lynching; bombing; the
> wanton and capricious murder of Blacks by whites. As long as
> there are human beings, there will be problems in relation-
> ships.
> Life is not a problem similar to science or mathematics where
> solutions can be discerned and tested. Life is a process where
> people mix and match, fall apart and come back together. We
> hope, we continue. Our soul is rested, but it will have to get up
> in the morning and start again (1994, 40–41).

The Art Connection

Several of Nikki Giovanni's poems have been turned into picture
books: *Knoxville, Tennessee* (1994), illustrated by Larry Johnson,
The Genie in the Jar (1996), illustrated by Chris Raschka, *The Sun
Is So Quiet: Poems* (1996), illustrated by Ashley Bryan. Have stu-
dents choose a poem of Nikki Giovanni's that they think would
appeal to young readers and then create a picture book illustrat-
ing its images and ideas. I like to provide students with blank
books to work in. These don't cost much—usually no more than
a dollar each (Bare Books, Inc.) and are well worth the invest-
ment as students can focus on the illustrations and placement of
Giovanni's lines rather than on binding pages. For students who
consider themselves artistically challenged, encourage them to
use pictures from magazines or to take photographs of their own
to provide illustration for Giovanni's words.

Have students include in their book both a short author-bio-
graphy of Nikki Giovanni and a biographical reference for them-

selves as illustrators. I allow students to take some poetic license with their own but require that they include a small photo of themselves. As students read one another's illustrated books, you can teach them about book jacket blurbs and have them write these for one another's books. "A masterpiece! My child asks for this book night after night." "The bright illustrations make Giovanni's simple words light up the page." "A must read!"

Two particularly good sources for Nikki Giovanni poetry suitable for children are *Spin a Black Song* (1987) and *Ego-Tripping and Other Poems for Young People* (1993). Both are in print and available in paperback editions.

The Music Connection

Nikki Giovanni herself has often included music in her poetry readings, either as background for the reading or as actual accompaniment to individual lines. Ask students to pick a poem of Giovanni's that they feel has particularly strong rhythm and plan a performance of this poem using music. I find that this assignment works best when students collaborate in small groups.

If you can stand the noise, borrow a set of percussion instruments from the music department. (I have a set of my own but can only bear to bring them into class once or twice a school year.) As students experiment with sounds and rhythms for their poems, question them about the reasons behind their musical choices. As part of the performance, one person in each group should explain the genesis of the group's interpretation.

6 More . . .

■ ■

If I could own only one book by Nikki Giovanni, it would be her collection *The Selected Poems of Nikki Giovanni* published by William Morrow and Company (1996). Most "selected poems" volumes are published because a poet's early books have gone out of print. This is not the case with Giovanni, but I still find it enormously valuable to have selections from six of her books gathered in one place. The collection also offers a clear record of Giovanni's evolution as a writer. Buy it for yourself as a birthday present.

For students, I love to use the slim, individual volumes of poetry. To me no classroom library is complete without the following collections of Nikki Giovanni poetry:

- *Black Feeling, Black Talk, Black Judgement,* paperback. 1979. New York: Morrow Quill Paperbacks. Reprinted in 1989.
- *Cotton Candy on a Rainy Day,* paperback. 1978. New York: Morrow Quill Paperbacks. Reprinted in 1989.
- *Ego-Tripping and Other Poems for Young People,* paperback. 1993. Chicago: Lawrence Hill Books.
- *Love Poems,* 1997. New York: William Morrow.
- *My House Poems,* paperback. 1974. New York: William Morrow.
- *Spin a Soft Black Song,* paperback. 1987. New York: Hill & Wang.

- *Those Who Ride the Night Winds*, paperback. 1983. New York: William Morrow.
- *The Women and the Men*, paperback. 1970. New York: William Morrow.

Other, Highly Recommended Works by Nikki Giovanni

Gemini, An Extended Autobiographical Statement on My First Twenty-Five Years of Being a Black Poet, Nikki Giovanni, 1976. New York: Viking Press. First published in 1971.

Written when Giovanni was twenty-five years old, this collection of autobiographical essays offers a record of the 1960s in America. Giovanni interweaves warm recollections from her own personal history with incisive vignettes of the times she lived through. She chronicles the changing moods of society while revealing the inner and outer worlds of a black woman in twentieth-century America.

A Poetic Equation, Conversations between Nikki Giovanni and Margaret Walker. 1983. Washington, D.C.: Howard University Press. First published in 1974.

In 1972 both Nikki Giovanni and Margaret Walker were invited to read at the Paul Laurence Dunbar Centennial at the University of Dayton. This is an informal book, tapings of two conversations, but intense. There are many places where the discussion becomes emotionally heated because the two women possess different sensibilities. The recurring theme which threads through the book is the destiny of the people who find themselves in the eye of the racial storm in America. This book is an uninhibited dialogue between two women a generation apart, a mother-daughter confrontation in the spirit of love and respect.

Shimmy Shimmy Shimmy Like My Sister Kate: Looking at the Harlem Renaissance through Poems, edited by Nikki Giovanni. 1996. New York: Henry Holt & Company.

In this book designed with a young adult audience in mind, Nikki Giovanni celebrates the flowering of African American poetry during the Harlem Renaissance. Her informal commentary that follows each poem offers young readers insight into her own love for words and for these poets. The final paragraph reads, "I think that we're lucky that we're still living with the influence of a people who believed that if we could write a poem, if we could sing a song—I suppose if we were looking at it today, if we could make a rap—if we could find a way to tell people that we, too, have dreams, they would honor our humanness. I think that's a great calling. I think it's something we need to be very proud of."

Grand Mothers: Poems, Reminiscences, and Short Stories about the Keepers of Our Traditions, edited by Nikki Giovanni. 1994. New York: Henry Holt & Company.

As Nikki Giovanni states in her introduction, "This isn't a balanced book nor a sociological book nor a look at grandmothers through the ages. It's just a book that makes me miss the only person I know for sure whose love I did not have to earn." The volume includes contributions from poets, novelists, and civil rights leaders, honoring their grandmothers and traditions. As a whole it demonstrates what a crucial role elder women play in carrying traditions across generations. Contributors include Gwendolyn Brooks, Kyoko Mori, Gloria Naylor, and Maxine Hong Kingston.

Racism 101, Nikki Giovanni. 1994. New York: William Morrow.

This collection of short essays offers insights, opinions, and a survival guide for black students on predominantly white college campuses. She frequently evokes the memories and lessons of the sixties as evidence of gains in justice and equality for black Americans. But with racism still present in both society and the classroom, Giovanni comes down hard on higher education for the inequities it perpetrates. Whether or not you agree with her analysis, you can always count on Nikki Giovanni to speak her mind.

Recordings

Four recordings by Nikki Giovanni of her own work are currently available on CD:

- *In Philadelphia,* 1997.

- *Way I Feel,* 1995. This recording includes "My House," "The Way I Feel," "When I Die," "Revolutionary Dreams," and "The Life I Led."

- *Like a Ripple on a Pond,* 1993. This recording includes "Legacies," "Pass Me Not," Deep River," "Africa II," "Like a Ripple on a Pond," and "I'm Glad."

- *Truth Is on Its Way,* 1993. This recording includes "Nikki Rosa," "Alabama Poem," "Ego-Tripping," "Woman Poem," and "Poem for a Lady of Leisure Now Retired."

Nikki on the Net

Nikki Giovanni's homepage is http://athena.english.vt.edu/Giovanni/Nikki_Giovanni.html

Works Cited

FOWLER, VIRGINIA. 1994. Foreword to *Racism 101*, by Nikki Giovanni. New York: William Morrow.

GIOVANNI, NIKKI. 1994. "I Plant Geraniums." *Racism 101*. New York: William Morrow.

————. 1994. "The Sixties." *Racism 101*. New York: William Morrow.

————. 1989. "Writing as Breathing, Nikki Giovanni." *Writer's Digest*: 30–34.

————. 1969. "On Being Asked What It's Like to Be Black." *US*. October 1969: 94–101.

————. 1994. "Meatloaf: a View of Poetry." *Racism 101*. New York: William Morrow.

————. 1997. *Love Poems*. New York: William Morrow.

LEWIS, IDA. 1983. Foreword to *My House*, by Nikki Giovanni. New York: William Morrow.

NATIONAL COUNCIL OF TEACHERS OF ENGLISH, speech given at the 1998 Annual Convention, Nashville, TN.

OLIVER, MARY. 1998. *Rules for the Dance: A Handbook for Writing and Reading Metrical Verse*. Boston: Houghton Mifflin.

PERRINE, LAURENCE. 1991. *Sound and Sense*. San Diego, CA: Harcourt Brace.

SCHLEIER, CURT. 1996. "Versed in Protest." *The Detroit News*. March 7, 1996.

Author

Carol Jago teaches English at Santa Monica High School in Santa Monica, California, and directs the California Reading and Literature Project at UCLA. She is editor of *California English*, the quarterly journal of the California Association of Teachers of English (CATE). Jago also writes a weekly education column for the *Los Angeles Times*. Her essays have appeared in *English Journal, Language Arts, NEA Today, The Christian Science Monitor*, and other newspapers across the nation. She has been director of the NCTE Commission on Literature and currently serves on the Secondary Section of the Executive Committee of the National Council of Teachers of English.

This book was composed by Electronic Imaging.

The typeface used on the cover was Interstate Regular Condensed.

The book was printed on 60-lb. opaque paper by Versa Press.